E-learning and training in Europe

A survey into the use of e-learning
in training and professional development
in the European Union

Cedefop Reference series; 26

Luxembourg: Office for Official Publications of the European Communities, 2001

A great deal of additional information on the European Union is available on the Internet. It can be accessed through the Europa server (http://europa.eu.int).

Cataloguing data can be found at the end of this publication.

Luxembourg:
Office for Official Publications of the European Communities, 2002

ISBN 92-896-0106-X
ISSN 1608-7089

Designed by Colibri Ltd. – Greece
Printed in Greece

The **European Centre for the Development of Vocational Training** (Cedefop) is the European Union's reference Centre for vocational education and training. We provide information on and analyses of vocational education and training systems, policies, research and practice. Cedefop was established in 1975 by Regulation (EEC) No. 337/75 of the Council.

Europe 123
GR-570 01 Thessaloniki (Pylea)

Postal address: PO Box 22427
GR-551 02 Thessaloniki

Tel. (30) 310 490 111, Fax (30) 310 490 020
E-mail: info@cedefop.eu.int
Homepage: www.cedefop.eu.int
Interactive website: www.trainingvillage.gr

In cooperation with:
Terry Ward, *Alphametrics Ltd.*
Tim Harrison, *Alphametrics Ltd.*
with the assistance of Jane Massy

Edited by: **Cedefop**
Colin Mc Cullough, *Project Coordinator*
Eva Smirli, *Surveys Coordinator*

Published under the responsibility of:
Johan van Rens, *Director*
Stavros Stavrou, *Deputy Director*

Table of contents

Introduction

Background

E-learning has the potential to change education and training radically, to open new ways of teaching and to increase the ability of people to acquire new skills. Its development is important for governments looking to widen access to education and training and to increase the qualifications of those entering the labour market and for companies seeking new business opportunities or to maintain or strengthen their competitiveness through continuously improving productivity.

E-learning has created new markets for teaching and learning material and equipment, attracting the attention of academic institutions as well as companies supplying them in different sectors – computer manufacturers, software producers, publishing houses and special training providers. It has also led to the reorientation of government policy, in the European Union (EU) in particular, towards encouraging the spread of e-learning techniques and developing the skills and know-how required for their use.

Therefore, e-learning was assigned a key role in the pursuit of the EU's policy objective, announced at the Lisbon Summit in March 2000, of making the EU 'the most competitive and dynamic knowledge-driven economy in the world'. The e-learning initiative was launched by the European Commission two months later to encourage its spread. This was followed by its incorporation into the European employment strategy in the form of a specific objective of 'developing e-learning for all citizens'. To achieve this, EU Member States committed themselves to ensuring that 'all education and training institutions have access to the Internet and multimedia resources by the end of 2001 and that all the teachers and trainers concerned are skilled in the use of these technologies by the end of 2002 in order to provide all pupils with a broad digital literacy' (Guideline 5, Employment Guidelines, 2001).

Despite its central importance in government policy and significant interest in the scale of the actual and potential market, there is an acute shortage of quantitative information on the extent of e-learning in providing initial and continuing vocational education and training and on the rate at which it is growing.

Although some surveys have been carried out on the size of the market and its rate of growth, many of these are of questionable reliability since the size and representative nature of the sample on which they are based are invariably difficult to discern. Those not confined to a single country often focus on large multinational companies, especially US ones and particularly those in the information and communication technology (ICT) sector. While unquestionably of importance these are by no means the sole or possibly even the main source of demand or supply. They also tend to treat the European market as a single entity without drawing any distinction between different countries or different subject areas.

This lack of hard evidence makes it difficult for governments, companies and other organisations to develop coherent and effective policies in this area. It makes it equally difficult for governments to assess the effectiveness of the measures introduced and the expenditure incurred and determine the action needed if the strategic objectives to encourage the spread of e-learning are to be achieved.

Although fairly straightforward to collect information from schools and colleges on the PCs and other multimedia they own and their access to the Internet and the exposure of pupils and students to e-learning techniques, it is much harder to compile similar information outside the mainstream education sector. To ascertain the extent and pace of developing e-learning in vocational education and training is far more complicated since the training market in Europe is highly fragmented and involves a huge variety of different players, private as well as public.

Aims of the survey

This report is the product of a study aimed at investigating the feasibility of collecting data on the use of e-learning methods in vocational education and training in the EU.

Its specific focus was on initial and continuing vocational education and training – i.e. the training provided to those in employment or seeking to return to work to extend or update their skills and knowledge – rather than on education.

The sample of companies and organisations covered is fairly small, particularly in some countries, even if larger than most previous surveys in this area. The survey is not scientifically based in the sense of covering a representative number of players in each part of the market. While it is impossible to ascertain how far the respondents from whom replies were received are representative of the organisations involved in vocational education and training, whether as suppliers or users, they, nevertheless, include different types and sizes of organisation from all EU countries. Therefore, the survey can claim to give a more comprehensive view about e-learning in the EU and its rate of development than has been available up to now.

Despite being kept deliberately short to maximise the response rate, the questionnaire covered the main points at issue: the use of e-learning in relation to other forms and methods of training in different subject areas; the extent to which suppliers of e-learning tend also to be users; the importance of e-learning as a source of income for training providers and as en element of expenditure for users compared with other training activities; and the growth of the e-learning market in terms of the revenue generated and the spending incurred.

Definition of e-learning

Although there is a tendency to equate e-learning with the use of the Internet for teaching purposes, this seems too narrow a conception of the term, since much the same training programmes are often provided either on an Internet website or on CD-ROM or a combination of the two. The definition of e-learning adopted here is that adopted by Cedefop since 2000. It is a rather broad one, namely:

'learning that is supported by information and communication technologies (ICT). E-learning is, therefore, not limited to 'digital literacy' (the acquisition of IT competence) but may encompass multiple formats and hybrid methodologies, in particular, the use of software, Internet, CD-ROM, online learning or any other electronic or interactive media.'

Key considerations – the distinctive features of the study

The starting point of the study, which distinguishes it from most other surveys conducted in this area, was the recognition that, if meaningful results were to be obtained, it was important to differentiate between:

- **different countries and languages**; the most obvious difference between European countries is that of language; this tends to affect the rate at which e-learning is taken up, if only because much of the content of new programmes has initially been in English, reflecting that most suppliers come from North America. Countries with English as a native language or with high levels of second language English speakers (the Netherlands, Denmark, Finland and Sweden, in particular) have obviously been targeted first by e-learning suppliers. Language, however, is not the most critical difference;

- **different vocational education and training systems in Europe;** more importantly, each country has its own vocational education and training system. While having certain aspects in common with systems elsewhere, each tends to have its own distinctive national features which reflect economic, social and cultural characteristics as well as the system's evolution and the broad institutional context in which it operates. These distinctive national features are likely to affect the development of e-learning in different parts of Europe – the way in which e-learning is incorporated into training and the pace at which this happens. In practice it will tend to take longer for e-learning techniques to be incorporated into vocational education and training in a country such as Germany, which has a highly structured system and where the possibility of pursuing a particular vocation depends on completing a well-defined programme of training, than in a country like the UK, where the system is much less structured;

- **different types of organisation**; there are a range of players involved in providing vocational education and training. These need to be separately distinguished if a representative picture is to be obtained. Since there is no officially recognised system in Europe for classifying training providers into distinct categories, an initial task of the study was to devise such a classifi-

cation system which was not only specific to the study but which could serve more generally. The types of organisation distinguished were as follows:
- university/college of further or higher education,
- public vocational education and training organisation,
- sector/industry training body (organised by professional/trade association, trade union),
- voluntary or social organisation,
- private training company/organisation,
- private or public organisation (any sector) with internal training services,
- private or public organisation (any sector) with internal and external training services,
- organisation specialising in producing/providing training tools/content,
- other type of organisation;

- **users and providers of training**; the demand and supply sides of the market for e-learning, since they may behave differently and display different trends at this stage of early development, need to be distinguished from each other. Such a distinction, however, is too simplistic because consumers or users of training are often both suppliers and providers simultaneously. Indeed, one of the main findings of the study is that many organisations buying in training from outside are also training providers, either supplying training internally within the organisation itself or externally to other organisations;

- **different subject areas**; many e-learning surveys conducted in the past concentrated on the use of such methods in the training of information and communication technology; while this is undoubtedly one of the main areas of application, it is important to investigate the development of e-learning in other subject areas, such as language learning, acquiring other technical skills or in management, where its potential could be equally large if not greater;

- **current and capital spending**; the distinction between current spending, or expenditure on training content, and capital spending, or the investment in equipment required to receive or provide e-learning, is often blurred. But it is important to separate the two if data on the amount spent on e-learning are to be meaningfully interpreted. In practice, a significant proportion of spending on e-learning so far has gone on hardware and infrastructure rather than on software, the content of e-learning programmes tending to lag behind the capacity of hardware systems and the Internet to deliver.

The form of the survey

The survey was conducted via the Internet, by a web-based questionnaire (hosted on the European Training Village –ETV– website: www.trainingvillage.gr). This was carefully designed to elicit information on key aspects while being as easy and quick to complete as possible to obtain the maximum response rate. The issues addressed concerned:
- the types of organisation involved in e-learning and their size;
- whether they are providers or users of e-learning or both;
- the importance of e-learning in relation to classroom tuition;
- the use of e-learning in different subject areas;
- the amount spent by users on e-learning compared to other forms of training over the last three years;
- the revenue earned by providers over the same period.

To increase the response rate the questionnaire was translated into French, German and Spanish. A copy of the questionnaire is included as an annex to this report, together with more details of how the survey was carried out.

Requests to complete the survey (with follow-up reminders) were circulated to as many organisations involved in training as possible. Cedefop's own substantial contact database was supplemented by an extensive search to identify other databases and lists of participants in training provision in different parts of Europe.

It is inevitable that conducting the survey in this way is likely to bias the results, in the sense that it was confined to those with access to the Internet, who are more likely to use e-learning training methods or to supply training in this form. It was also limited to organisations with an expressed interest in training, as they were included in Cedefop or other databases or in lists of training providers.

Nevertheless, it is unlikely that a great number of training providers or significant users do not have access to the Internet, so the degree of bias revealed by the form of the survey may not be large. Although it would have been desirable to complement the web-based survey with a traditional, paper-based approach, assuming this would have produced a significant response, the aim was to create the basis for a repeatable survey of developments in the future. Use of the worldwide web for the survey was considered an important feature in itself.

1. Respondents to the survey

1.1. Coverage of countries

A total of 800 completed questionnaires were received in the survey. Of these, 653 were from organisations based in the EU and another 89 from other parts of Europe. This report is based on the replies received from organisations in the EU, though it is encouraging that some 62 replies were received from candidate countries, which were not specifically targeted.

The replies from the EU covered all 15 Member States, and apart from Luxembourg (from which there were five replies), the smallest number received was from Austria, for which 19 questionnaires were completed. The Austrian respondents, however, represented just under 3 % of total replies, which is slightly larger than Austria's share of the total work force in the EU (just over 2 %), which seems an appropriate benchmark to take to assess the relative scale of coverage. The overall provision of training in each country, in other words, ought to correspond roughly to the size of its labour force (i.e. the number in employment plus the number unemployed and looking for work).

Figure 1: **Distribution of responses to the survey and share of EU labour force by Member State**

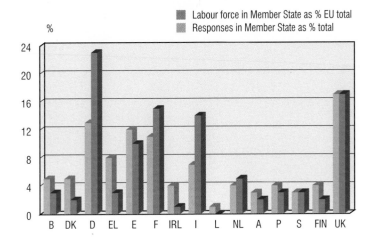

Given this approximate correspondence, comparing the distribution of replies between EU Member States with their share of the EU workforce not only gives an indication of the relative coverage of the survey, but also provides a possible insight into differences between countries in their interest in e-learning and its importance in vocational education and training (Figure 1). The tentative nature of any conclusions drawn from this comparison, however, needs to be emphasised.

From this perspective, the first point to note is that although more replies were received from the UK than elsewhere, amounting to around 16.5 % of the total, the proportion was slightly less than the UK's share of the EU workforce (17 %).

Secondly, the number of replies from Denmark, Finland, Ireland and Greece was considerably larger than expected given the size of their workforce in each case. This might be indicative of the interest in e-learning in those countries.

Thirdly, at the opposite extreme, the number of replies received from Italy was only half as many expected given the size of its workforce. This might be attributable to the questionnaire not being translated into Italian.

Fourthly, the proportion of replies from Germany and France, the former in particular, was also less than their share of the EU workforce despite the questionnaire being available in these languages. This contrasts with Spain, which was slightly above its share of the EU workforce. There is no clear explanation for these differences.

1.2. The types of organisation supplying information

Figure 2: Division of responses by type of organisation

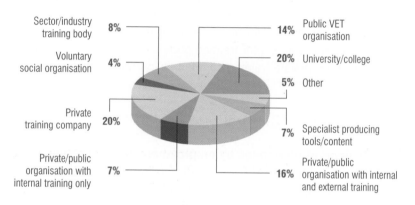

The survey elicited responses from the full range of organisation types distinguished above. The largest number were received from private training companies, which accounted for just over 19 % of the total, though only a slightly smaller number were received from universities and colleges (Figure 2). Companies or public sector organisations not specialising in training, but providing training externally as well as internally, accounted for around 15 % of the total. Public sector vocational education and training organisations, other than those in the education sector, represented another 14 %.

For the rest, a similar proportion of responses came from sector or industry training bodies (just over 7 %), companies specialising in producing training tools or content (7 %) and companies or organisations involved only in providing internal training (just over 6 %). Voluntary organisations accounted for 4 % of the total and others for just under 5 %. The smallness of the latter figure shows the comparative success of the classification system devised, in that almost all respondents were able to identify a suitable category in which to include themselves. The 'other' category included, for example, consultants, examination boards, training networks and international organisations, most of which could probably be classified in one or other of the named categories, though few of them were involved in e-learning either as a user or provider.

The relative number of replies received from different types of organisation in individual Member States was broadly similar. For most countries, the survey covered a wide range of training providers. It is risky to draw any firm conclusions on the relative importance of different types of provider in individual Member States from the number of replies received, which may simply reflect their presence on lists of providers or their willingness to complete a questionnaire. Nevertheless, it may be indicative that a larger than average proportion of the replies were from public-sector vocational education and training organisations in the three Nordic countries and Belgium, the Netherlands, Ireland and Austria, from sector training bodies in Denmark, the Netherlands and Spain, or from private training companies in France, Italy and Ireland.

1.3. The size of organisations responding

Figure 3: **Division of responses by employment size of organisation**

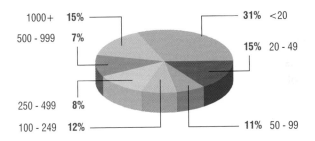

1000+ **15%**	**31%** <20
500 - 999 **7%**	**15%** 20 - 49
250 - 499 **8%**	
100 - 249 **12%**	**11%** 50 - 99

The survey covered different sizes of organisation providing training. Some 18 % of those giving figures had a turnover of over EUR 20 million, while 17 % had a turnover of under EUR 1 million. For employment, which gives a more reliable indication of size, if only because 94 % of respondents provided information, around 22 % of organisations had 500 or more employees and 15 %, 1000 or more. Not all of these employees are directly involved in providing training. At the other end of the scale, some 31 % had fewer than 20 and a further 15 % or so had between 20 and 49 employees. It is the response from these smaller organisations, in particular, which demarcates the survey from most other previous ones which have concentrated on large companies or academic institutions (Figure 3).

Figure 4: **Division of responses by employment size of organisation in Member States**

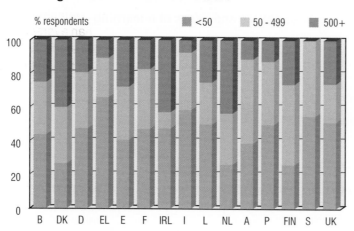

Again, it is difficult to draw firm conclusions from the replies received about the size of organisations involved in training provision in different Member States. Because of lack of general information, however, it is interesting to note that the proportion of responses from organisations with under 50 employees was highest in Greece and Italy (where small firms account for a larger share of total employment in the economy than elsewhere in the EU). At the same time, a higher proportion of replies came from large organisations in Denmark, the Netherlands and Ireland than elsewhere (Figure 4).

For types of organisation, most replies received from both private training providers and companies specialising in producing training tools or content were from small companies. Some 78 % of the latter had fewer than 50 employees and 60 % fewer than 20, while 75 % of training providers employed under 50 and 57 % under 20. Only around 7 % of both types of organisation had 500 or more employees. This is a reasonable reflection of the size of such companies. Indeed, the relative number of replies received from companies of different sizes was similar in most Member States. Only in Spain, were fewer than half the replies from private training providers from companies with under 50 employees (though only 7 % were from those with 500 or more). In the UK, the figure was over 90 %. Similarly, 60 % or more of replies from companies specialising in tools or content in all Member States were from those with under 50 employees.

On the other hand, many universities or colleges and organisations providing internal training only, employed significant numbers of people (over 40 % in both cases employed 500 or more and most of these 1 000 or more).

1.4. Suppliers and users of training

Figure 5: Division of suppliers and users of e-learning

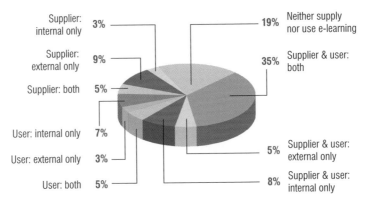

Supplier: internal only 3%
Supplier: external only 9%
Supplier: both 5%
User: internal only 7%
User: external only 3%
User: both 5%
19% Neither supply nor use e-learning
35% Supplier & user: both
5% Supplier & user: external only
8% Supplier & user: internal only

Just over 80 % of the organisations responding to the survey were either suppliers or users of e-learning. Almost 20 % were not involved in e-learning at all, despite being either training providers or consumers (Figure 5). Perhaps the most striking point is that nearly half of the respondents, 60 % of all those involved in e-learning, were both suppliers and users. E-learning is similar to the market for academic literature, where authors of books and journals sold also make up a significant proportion of buyers. Like the academic publishing market, this characteristic reflects the high degree of specialisation in particular areas which prevails, combined with the continuous development of knowledge and know-how which needs to be assimilated. Unlike this market, it also reflects the wide range of tasks which are typically performed in any individual organisation, each of which may be differentially affected by the advance of knowledge and technology, making it difficult for any organisation to keep abreast of developments and new possibilities without recourse to external expertise.

The other 40 % of organisations involved in e-learning were evenly split between suppliers only (21 %) and users only (19 %). Most suppliers (80 % or so), whether also users of e-learning or not, provided training to external users. Most suppliers were also involved in internal training. Equally, most organisations which were users of e-learning purchased or obtained training from external providers, besides most of them receiving training internally.

1.5. Differences between Member States

**Figure 6: Distribution of suppliers and users
of vocational education and training by Member State**

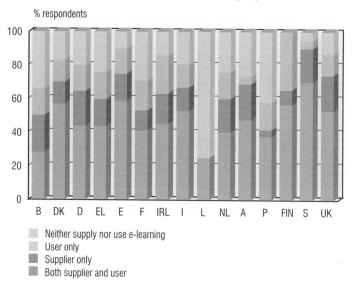

% respondents

Neither supply nor use e-learning
User only
Supplier only
Both supplier and user

The proportion of respondents not involved in e-learning, either as users or suppliers, varied significantly between EU countries. In Finland, no organisation fell into this category and in Sweden, only 5 %. In Portugal, however, over 40 % did, as did over a third in Belgium, almost 30 % in France and Austria and around a quarter in Greece (Figure 6). This is indicative of the less extensive use of e-learning techniques in the latter countries.

In all countries, except Belgium, most users of e-learning were also suppliers, the proportion reaching almost 75 % in Sweden and nearly 70 % in Denmark.

1.6. Suppliers and users by size

Figure 7: Division of organisations by employment size

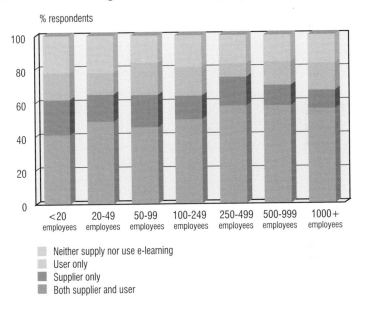

The results of the survey suggest that larger organisations involved in vocational education and training are more likely to make use of e-learning than smaller ones. While over 22 % of respondents with fewer than 50 employees made no use at all of e-learning, the figure for those with 500 or more employees was under 17 % (Figure 7). Equally, large organisations are also more likely to be both users and suppliers of e-learning, 68 % of respondents employing 500 or more falling into this category, against 61 % of those with 50 to 499 employees and 56 % of those employing under 50 people.

1.7. Suppliers and users by type of organisation

Figure 8: Types of organisation by employment size

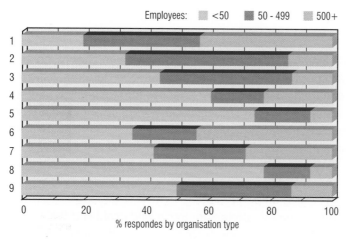

1 University/college
2 Public vocational education and training organisation
3 Sector training body
4 Voluntary/social organisation
5 Private training company
6 Private/public organisation with internal training
7 Private/public organisation with intenal and external training
8 Specialist tools/content company
9 Other

The survey suggests that a larger proportion of specialist companies producing training tools or content make use of e-learning than other types of organisation. Indeed almost all such companies (91 %) replying to the survey used e-learning (Figure 8). Almost as large a proportion of organisations (just over 90 %), whether public or private, providing only internal training also made use of e-learning, which was more than for companies specialising in training provision (85 %), for which the figure was much the same as for universities and colleges. Public sector vocational education and training organisations and industry or sector training bodies are least likely to be involved in e-learning. Nevertheless, only just over 20 % of respondents in these two categories did not use e-learning at all for training.

According to the survey, of those involved in e-learning, universities and colleges were most likely to be suppliers as well as users (72 % of respondents), followed by public vocational education and training organisations and industry or sector training boards (63 %), while only just over 55 % of private training providers were both users and suppliers.

2. Methods of training delivery

The use of e-learning for training has sometimes been portrayed as an alternative to classroom teaching, not least in marketing literature, which has often presented e-learning as a more cost-effective form of training than traditional methods. However, it is also arguable that e-learning should not be regarded so much an alternative to the classroom but a complement to it, making such teaching more effective not only in cost terms but also in quality and results. Multimedia tools have the capacity to improve traditional teaching methods, enrich the content and experience of training courses and increase the potential impact of learning on performance.

Although e-learning is important for those who might find it difficult to attend formal courses by making it easier for them to study alone and at their own pace it does not necessarily render the classroom less important. Indeed, to see the two as alternatives, is to adopt too narrow a view of e-learning, by regarding it merely as a means of mirroring what happens in the classroom, or a substitute for direct contact with a teacher or trainer, instead of a complement which increases their potential effectiveness.

Figure 9: **Suppliers of training by time spent on e-learning and in classroom tuition in Member States**

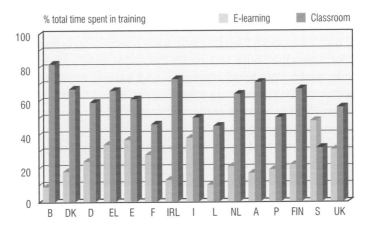

Figure 10: **Users of training by time spent on e-learning and classroom tuition in Member States**

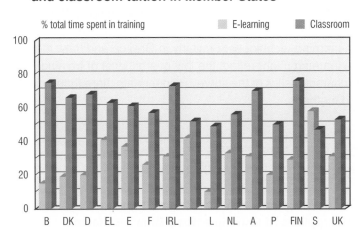

In practice, the survey shows that most training is still delivered through the classroom. The proportion of time spent in the classroom when providing or receiving training remains fairly high throughout the EU. Taking all respondents together, around 60 % of the overall amount of time devoted to training, among both users and suppliers, was spent in the classroom (Figures 9 and 10). The proportion, however, varied markedly across the EU, from over 70 % for both suppliers and users in Belgium, Ireland and Austria and for users in Finland, to around half for both in Italy and Portugal and to under half for both in Sweden and for users in France.

At the same time, a significant proportion of time was spent on training through e-learning. For both users and providers replying to the survey, an average of around 30 % of the time absorbed by training involved e-learning. Again there was significant variation between Member States, from around half of training time in Sweden for both users and suppliers and around 40 % for users in Greece and Italy to only around 20 % in Portugal and Denmark, around 15 % for suppliers in Austria and Ireland and to under 10 % for suppliers in Belgium.

These figures need to be interpreted with caution. They reflect the overall amount of time devoted to vocational education and training – on practical, workplace or on-the-job training as well as the principles or theory of the subject being taught – both in conventional training environments and in e-learning. In the Nordic countries, the time devoted to vocational education and training both at the initial stage and on continuing training for those in employment is relatively high. In the southern Member States, especially in Greece and

Portugal, it is rather low. The small proportion of time spent by users on e-learning in Denmark might be more a reflection of the large amount of time devoted to training as a whole than of the low incidence of e-learning. In Portugal, as well as Belgium, it might be a more accurate reflection of the rather limited development of e-learning techniques. Similarly in Greece and Italy, the fairly high figures for e-learning might reflect the low overall level of training, as well as the specific characteristics of the survey respondents more than extensive use of e-learning methods.

2.1. Suppliers of training – the relative use of e-learning and the classroom

Figure 11: **Relationship between classroom tuition and e-learning for suppliers of training across Member States**

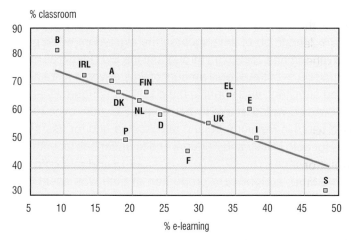

For suppliers of training, there is a clear negative relationship across EU countries between the proportion of time devoted to e-learning and that spent in the classroom. This suggests a substitution of the supply of training through e-learning for classroom delivery. In those Member States where a fairly large proportion of training is delivered through e-learning, the time devoted to classroom teaching is rather low and vice versa (Figure 11 – the correlation coefficient between the two proportions, which is a statistical measure of the relationship and can vary between 1 and −1 according to whether the association is positive or negative and its closeness, is −0.77).

Indeed, the relationship suggests that, on average, for every 10 percentage points by which the proportion of training delivered through e-learning is increased, the proportion provided through the classroom is reduced by around 9 percentage points. Imputing a causal relationship from this comparison across countries at one point in time, however, is risky, since it cannot necessarily be assumed the latter would follow if the former were to occur in any individual country.

Besides, there are several countries which diverge from the average relationship. In particular, in both Portugal and France, the proportion of training provided by e-learning is much less than expected given the fairly low proportion provided through the classroom. In Greece and Spain, more training is delivered through e-learning than would be expected given the high proportion of training in the classroom. In France, the explanation might lie in the strong bias towards personalisation of training and the challenge for suppliers of finding cost-effective solutions. In Greece and Spain, it appears the growth of e-learning has been less at the expense of classroom teaching than elsewhere. This may reflect an increase in training as a whole because of the growth of e-learning or in parallel with its development. An alternative interpretation is that in both countries, the use of the classroom for training is rather high because of the fairly small amount of time spent on practical training rather than because e-learning has been combined with a greater use of the classroom than in other countries.

2.2. Users of training – the relative use of e-learning and the classroom

Figure 12: Relationship between classroom tuition and e-learning for users of training across Member States

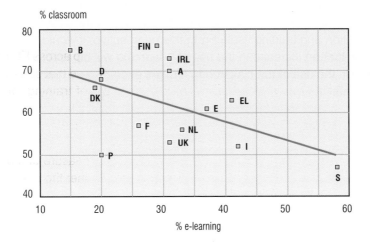

There is less of an association between the proportion of time spent on e-learning by those receiving training and that spent in the classroom, though the relationship between the two is still a negative one. Countries in which a rather high proportion of training received takes the form of e-learning have a smaller proportion of time spent in classroom tuition. However, there are more countries which diverge from the average relationship than with training providers (Figure 12 – the correlation coefficient in this case is -0.52).

Also, the trade-off between e-learning and classroom teaching is less proportionate than for training supply. The average relationship implies that for every 10 percentage points where there is an increase in the proportion of time spent using e-learning methods, the proportion of time sent in the classroom declines by just over four percentage points. Again it cannot necessarily be assumed from comparisons at one point in time that the latter would follow if the former occurred. Nevertheless, the replies to the survey suggest that users are less inclined than suppliers to substitute e-learning for classroom teaching and are perhaps looking for more 'blended' ways of integrating technology into training.

Finland, Ireland and Austria diverge from the average relationship. In all of them the use of e-learning is around the average for all respondents but this is combined with above average use of the classroom. Portugal, France and the UK diverge in the opposite direction. In all of these, a smaller proportion of time is spent in the classroom than would be expected given the time devoted to e-learning.

The one hard conclusion which can be drawn from the analysis is there are significant variations between countries in the relationship between e-learning and the classroom for users or recipients of training. Indeed, what appears to be a trade-off between e-learning and classroom methods may, in fact, not be a trade-off at all. It may simply be the reflection of different combinations of the two, which, in turn, might reflect national differences in the system of vocational education and training itself. From this perspective, it would not necessarily follow that an increase in the use of e-learning will be accompanied by a reduction in the use of the classroom. It might even be an expansion rather than a decline.

2.3. The use of e-learning and classroom methods by organisation size

Figure 13: Suppliers and users of training by time spent on e-learning and classroom tuition by size of organisation

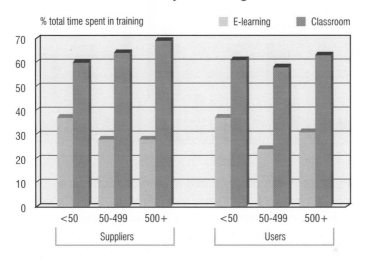

The survey shows that smaller organisations supplying training have adopted e-learning more than larger ones. Taking all the respondents together, almost 38 % of the training provided by those with under 50 employees involved the use of e-learning, whereas for larger organisations, the figure was only 28 % (Figure 13). Conversely, smaller organisations made less use of classroom-based training (this accounting for 60 % of the totals provided) than larger organisations (almost 69 % for those with 500 or more employees).

The differences were less pronounced for users. Small organisations employing fewer than 50 people made almost as much use of classroom-based training as large organisations employing 500 or more (61 % of time devoted to this by the former against 63 % by the latter). On the other hand, more training was received by small organisations through e-learning (37 %) than large organisations (31 %) or, more markedly, than medium-sized ones (24 %).

Figure 14: **Time spent on e-learning by training users by size of organisation**

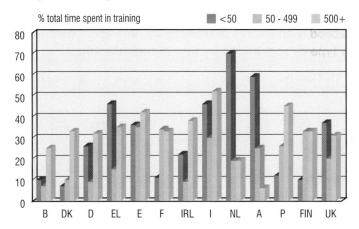

The same pattern was not repeated at Member State level. In nine of the 13 Member States for which there were replies from all size categories of organisation (i.e. excluding Luxembourg and Sweden), more use was made of e-learning in training in large organisations with 500 or more employees than in small ones (Figure 14). Only in Austria, Greece, the Netherlands and the UK was the reverse the case.

2.4. The use of e-learning and classroom methods by organisation type

Figure 15: Method of providing training by suppliers by type of organisation

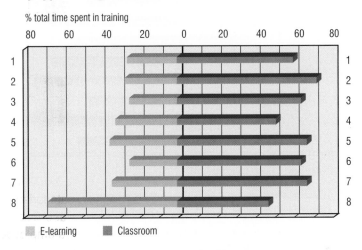

% total time spent in training

E-learning   Classroom

1 University/college, etc.
2 Public vocational education and training organisation
3 Sector/idustry training body
4 Voluntary/social organisation
5 Private training company
6 Private/public organisation with internal training only
7 Private/public organisation with intenal and external training
8 Specialist tools/content company

As expected, specialist companies producing tools or content devote more of their training effort to e-learning than other organisations involved in providing vocational education and training. For those replying to the survey, some two-thirds of the total training time delivered involved e-learning, compared with under half of the time spent in the classroom. Specialist companies were the only type of organisation for which this was the case (Figure 15). For other types of organisation, more than half the time was spent in the classroom and 25 % to 35 % in activities involving e-learning (35 % for private training companies, 25 % in the case of industry or sector training bodies).

Figure 16: **Users of training: time spent in e-learning and classroom tuition by type of organisation**

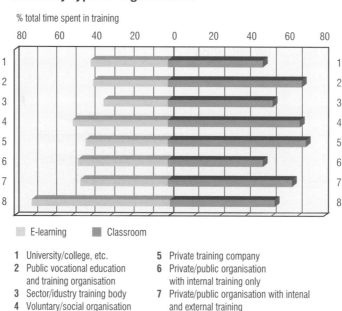

1 University/college, etc.
2 Public vocational education
   and training organisation
3 Sector/idustry training body
4 Voluntary/social organisation
5 Private training company
6 Private/public organisation
   with internal training only
7 Private/public organisation with intenal
   and external training
8 Specialist tools/content company

Specialist companies producing content also made more use of e-learning in the training they received than other types of organisation, over half of the time spent in training entailing e-learning in some form (Figure 16). In other types of organisation, apart from sector training bodies, around 30 % or more of training time involved e-learning.

2.5. The use of e-learning and classroom methods by subject area

Many studies of e-learning undertaken up to now have not made any distinction between subject areas of training, implicitly assuming they were all subject to the same development, or have concentrated on information and communication technology skills development. In practice, the survey shows that e-learning is extensively used in all areas of training, even if it is used more in information and communication technology than elsewhere.

Figure 17: Suppliers of training: time spent in e-learning and classroom tuition by subject area

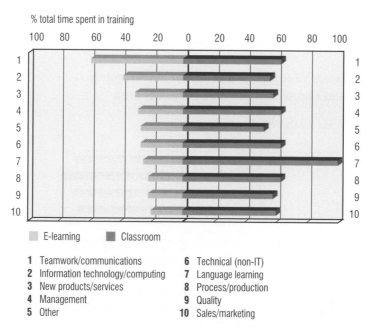

% total time spent in training

E-learning Classroom

1 Teamwork/communications
2 Information technology/computing
3 New products/services
4 Management
5 Other

6 Technical (non-IT)
7 Language learning
8 Process/production
9 Quality
10 Sales/marketing

According to the survey, some 38 % of the training for information and communication technology provided by suppliers involved e-learning (Figure 17). This, however, was less than for teamwork and communications, almost 60 % of the training for which entailed such methods. This is unexpected and difficult to explain. A possible explanation is the growth of cooperative learning platforms and their use in cooperative learning and working. By contrast, only 23 % of the training delivered by suppliers for sales and marketing involved e-learning, while only slightly more use was made of e-learning as a means of supporting process and production training and quality control training. Nevertheless, though lower than for other subject areas, these figures are still significant.

In all subject areas, over half the time devoted by suppliers to training was spent in classroom tuition. In teaching foreign languages, 100 % of the training provided was in the classroom (which might show that e-learning language providers were not well represented among the respondents). Apart from this, the variation in the proportion of training delivered in the classroom varied little between subjects (excluding the 'other' category, from just over 56 % for information and communication technology to just over 63 % for management).

There is no clear relationship between the proportion of time spent on e-learning and time spent in the classroom. There is, therefore, no evidence of any trade-off between the two across subject areas (the correlation coefficient is -0.11, which though showing a negative association, is not statistically significant).

Figure 18: **Users of training: time spent in e-learning and classroom tuition by subject area**

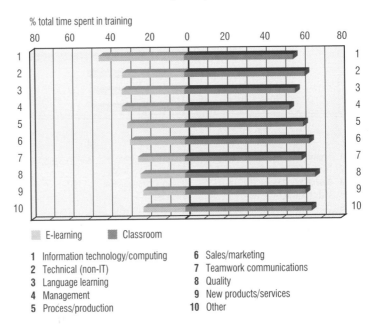

% total time spent in training

☐ E-learning   ■ Classroom

1 Information technology/computing
2 Technical (non-IT)
3 Language learning
4 Management
5 Process/production

6 Sales/marketing
7 Teamwork communications
8 Quality
9 New products/services
10 Other

Among users, the proportion of time spent on e-learning in different subject areas was similar to that for suppliers. This is to be expected, except for teamwork, on which much less time was spent using e-learning, and, to a lesser extent, for information and communication technology, where more time was spent using e-learning (43 % of the total time on training) (Figure 18). Similarly, as for suppliers, there was little variation in the relative amount of time spent by recipients of training in the classroom (ranging from 56 % for information and communication technology to 67 % for teamwork; in this case the time spent by those learning a foreign language in the classroom was much less than 100 %, presumably reflecting the time spent on self-tuition and practice).

Figure 19: **Relationship between time spent by users on e-learning and in classroom by subject area**

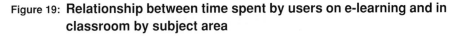
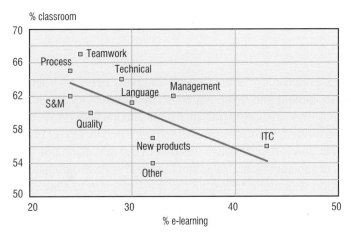

Unlike for suppliers, among users there is evidence of a negative relationship, and a possible trade-off, between the use made of e-learning and time spent in the classroom. The subjects in which rather high use was made of e-learning methods spent less time in the classroom (Figure 19 – the correlation coefficient in this case is -0.66). The relationship implies that for every 10 percentage points where the proportion of time spent on e-learning is above average, the proportion of time spent in the classroom is just over four percentage points below average. This, please note, is similar to the form of relationship for users of training across Member States mentioned above.

A final point to note is that training suppliers in each size of organisation made the same relative use of both e-learning and classroom tuition in different subject areas. In other words, for all sizes of organisation providing training, a higher proportion of time was spent on e-learning for teamwork than for any other subject, followed by information and communication technology, and the lowest use on sales and marketing, process and production and quality control.

However, in all subject areas, except for teamwork, significantly more use was made of e-learning by small organisations supplying training than by larger ones. Equally, in all subject areas, except information and communication technology and foreign language teaching (where 100 % of training was delivered in the classroom irrespective of the size of organisation), less use was made of the classroom by small organisations providing training than by large ones. This shows a high degree of consistency in the delivery of training within individual subject areas.

3. Growth of the e-learning market

The survey collected information on expenditure by users on training material and capital equipment and revenue earned by suppliers for providing material and equipment. The aim was to gain an insight into the importance of e-learning in the training market, for hardware and software and its rate of growth. There were, however, fewer responses to this part of the questionnaire. This is to be expected as organisations are reluctant to reveal sensitive details, although a conscious effort was made to design the questionnaire to allay concerns, by asking respondents to show revenue and costs in broad ranges rather than precise figures.

Some organisations were also only involved in internal training with no outside costs on training and no external income from it. Although internal training still involves costs, not all organisations can give a breakdown of these. Even when organisations purchase training from outside, this may not be readily distinguishable in their accounts. There may be similar difficulties for organisations delivering training as an integral part of the goods or services they provide. Similar difficulties apply to expenditure or revenue on e-learning. Indeed, it is likely to be even more problematic to identify the cost incurred on this or the income from providing it than training as a whole.

Nevertheless, financial information for the three years 1999 to 2001 was supplied by almost half the respondents, showing the split between e-learning and other methods of training and the change in expenditure and revenue over the period. This provides a reasonable view of the position and developments in these respects in eight EU Member States – the five largest countries and Greece, the Netherlands and Finland – as enough replies were received from organisations in these countries. Enough replies were also received to show differences between the various types and sizes of organisation involved in training.

At the same time, because data were collected in broad ranges rather than precise figures, the changes calculated are approximate. Little significance should be attached to small variations from year to year.

It should also be stressed that, much more than other parts of the survey, the data collected on revenue and expenditure reflect the timing of the enquiry. The data were collected during 2001, before September when economic prospects in the EU, already adversely affected by the downturn in the US, deteriorated further. The figures provided for 2001 are, therefore, estimates for the year, which will be affected to varying degrees by respondents' assessment of the impact of prevailing economic circumstances on their organisations.

3.1. Revenue from e-learning at EU level

Figure 20: E-learning as a share of revenue from the supply of training material and equipment in the EU

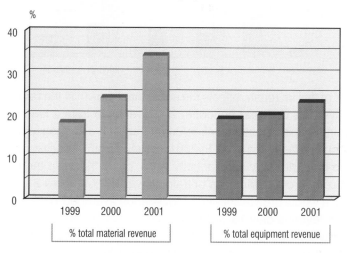

E-learning accounted for around a third of total revenue from providing training material in 2001 by suppliers responding to the survey (Figure 20). 'Training material' here excludes the supply of capital equipment of one kind or another and relates to program content delivered in the form, for example, of CD-ROMs or online or Internet-based services. This was markedly higher than two years previously in 1999, when only just over 18 % of total revenue from training material was produced by e-learning. (The analysis here is confined to respondents giving data for adjacent years, which understates growth as the increase resulting from new entrants to the training market over the period is excluded. Equally, the fall caused by organisations leaving the market, because they shifted their area of specialisation or went out of business, is also excluded. This will overstate market growth, though in this case, there are likely to have been more entrants than exits – at least up to September 2001).

Figure 21: **Growth of revenue from the supply of e-learning and other training material and equipment in the EU, 1999-2001**

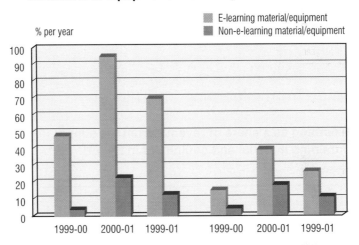

The scale of this increase reflects the substantial growth in the revenue from e-learning over this two-year period. In 2000, revenue from e-learning material by respondents increased by 48 % compared with an increase of just 4 % in non-e-learning-based material. In 2001, revenue from e-learning material is estimated to have risen by substantially more, by 95 %, while the estimated growth in income from other kinds of training was 23 % (Figure 21). Over the two years as a whole growth in e-learning revenue averaged 70 % a year, and other training revenue only 13 % a year.

E-learning was responsible for most of the increase in revenue from providing training over this period, despite it accounting for a fairly small part of the total income from training (under 20 % in 1999 and under a quarter in 2000). Over the two years e-learning accounted for over 60 % of the overall expansion of revenue.

The revenue from sales of hardware and infrastructure associated with e-learning was slightly smaller in relation to the total income of respondents from sales of capital equipment for training. In 2001, although 23 %, higher than two years earlier to just under 19 % of the total, this was much less of an increase than overall revenue from training material. Growth in revenue from e-learning-related sales of capital equipment over the two years averaged around 26 % a year.

3.2. Expenditure on e-learning at EU level

Figure 22: E-learning as a share of current and capital expenditure on training in the EU, 1999-2001

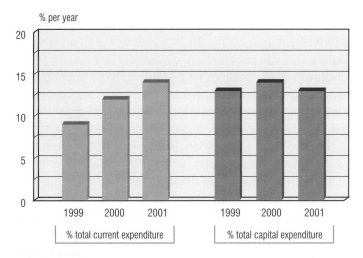

Training users responding to the survey spent just under 14 % of their total current (as opposed to capital) outlays on training on e-learning-related content in 2001. This was noticeably more than in 1999 when the figure was under 10 % (Figure 22).

Figure 23: Growth of expenditure on e-learning and other training material and equipment in the EU, 1999-2001

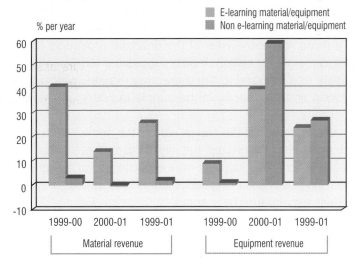

In 2000, expenditure on e-learning material by users increased by just over 40 %, while other current spending on training rose by only 3 %. In 2001 the growth in spending on e-learning was estimated at 14 %, significantly down on the preceding year (Figure 23). At the same time, current outlays on other forms of training fell slightly so there was still a marked shift in expenditure towards e-learning methods. Over the two years as a whole, spending on e-learning material went up by some 26 % a year whereas on other training, it rose only slightly.

This rate of growth of expenditure on e-learning, while substantial, is less than most previous surveys have suggested. There are two main reasons for this. The first is the present survey covers a wider range of organisations than most others have included, especially smaller firms and public bodies. Secondly, the survey was conducted at a time when economic conditions across the EU, and indeed globally, were deteriorating, when GDP growth was slowing and the prospects were for a downturn in the world economy, initiated by falling output in the US. E-learning cannot be expected to remain immune from such developments, even though it may represent a means of increasing the cost-effectiveness of training.

The difference between the estimate of suppliers of the likely revenue from providing e-learning material in 2001 and the estimate of users of the amount they were likely to spend on such material is significant. While the increase in revenue and expenditure in the preceding year was similar and suppliers in mid-2001 were anticipating a much higher growth of revenue than occurred the year before, users were expecting to spend less on e-learning material. Separate examination of the estimates of expenditure of public and private organisations (see below) shows the drop in estimates was more pronounced in the private than the public sector. This suggests that those responsible for purchasing had a more pessimistic – and, as it turned out, a more realistic – view of the financial prospects for the year than those responsible for selling. It also suggests a large-scale mismatch between supply and demand in the e-learning market, which could foreshadow growing spare capacity in the supply industry unless economic conditions improve.

The estimates of growth of the capital side of the market were much more similar, which may reflect the greater maturity of the market for equipment than that for content and services. Suppliers were expecting much the same increase in revenue from the sale of e-learning equipment in 2001 as users were expecting to increase their expenditure by – some 40 % or so (Figure 23). This was markedly higher than in 2000, when revenue from sales rose by just under 15 % and spending went up by around 9 %. While training users, therefore, were expecting to increase their expenditure on e-learning material by only a small extent, they were still envisaging a large increase in their spending on equipment.

3.3. Growth of revenue from e-learning in Member States

Figure 24: Growth of revenue from supply of e-learning material in Member States, 1999-2001

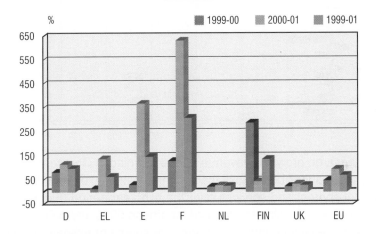

The survey shows that training providers in different Member States experienced differing patterns of sales growth over the two years 1999 to 2001. (Here the analysis is confined to suppliers of training content and services since the responses received on this part of the questionnaire from organisations supplying equipment and infrastructure – 75 in total – are too few to break down by country and get reliable results.) Although there was a distinct increase in the importance of e-learning as a source of revenue in all countries, the scale varied between them. The biggest increases in revenue from the supply of e-learning material over the two years taken together were in Finland, France, Germany and Spain, in each of which revenue growth was estimated to average around 100 % a year or more (Figure 24). In the last three of these, the increase in revenue in 2001 was expected to be substantially higher than in 2000. This was also the case in Greece, where revenue growth averaged 65 % a year, almost all of it concentrated in 2001. In the Netherlands and the UK growth averaged 25-30 % a year with a much more even distribution between the two years.

Figure 25: **Contribution of e-learning to overall growth of revenue from training material, 1999-2001**

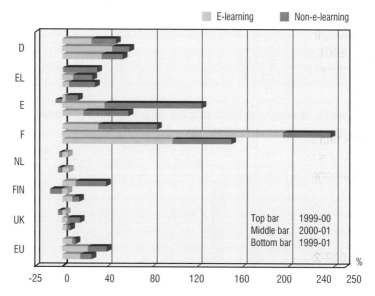

Despite the large growth in revenue from e-learning in Greece and Spain, e-learning was responsible for less than half the overall expansion in training revenue from content and services over the two-year period (Figure 25). In Finland, France and the UK, it accounted for around 55 % and in Germany for 65 %, while in the Netherlands, it was the sole source of revenue growth. In all countries, however, there was a marked rise over the two years in the relative importance of e-learning as a source of revenue.

3.4. Growth of expenditure on e-learning in Member States

As at EU level, in most Member States, growth of expenditure on e-learning material in 2001 estimated by training users was substantially lower than the rise in revenue estimated by suppliers. The main exception was Finland, where higher growth in spending was anticipated by users. Nationally, there is much less reason to expect consistency between estimates of market growth made by suppliers and users because of international trade in training material. Nevertheless, the fact there is a general tendency for users to be more pessimistic than suppliers is significant. It not only shows a more cautious attitude towards prospects among purchasers of e-learning than among suppliers but also, for the same reason, it implies the results produced by a survey of suppliers may give a different picture than a survey of users.

Figure 26: **Growth of expenditure on e-learning material in Member States, 1999-2001**

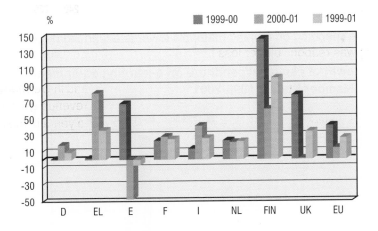

Over the two years 1999 and 2001, current, or material, spending on e-learning fell in Spain because of a large fall in 2001 (Figure 26). This was in marked contrast to the estimate noted above of a substantial growth in revenue from the supply of e-learning material. In Germany, where the estimate of revenue growth by suppliers was similarly high, spending increased by just 9 % a year over the period. In the other six countries for which there are reasonable data, the increase was much larger – over 20 % a year in the Netherlands, over 25 % a year in France and Italy and around 35 % a year in Greece and the UK, while in Finland, it doubled each year.

Figure 27: **Contribution of e-learning to overall growth of expenditure on training material, 1999-2001**

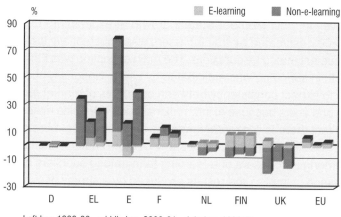

Left bar 1999-00, middle bar 2000-01, right bar 1999-01

In the UK, the large overall rise masks a very small rise in spending in 2001 (1.5 %), though this was accompanied by a much larger cut in other current outlays on training, so here, as in the other countries apart from Spain, there was a shift in spending on training materials towards e-learning (Figure 27).

Figure 28: **Growth of capital expenditure on e-learning equipment in Member States, 1999-2001**

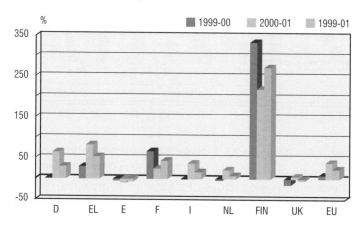

Expenditure on capital equipment relating to e-learning shows a different pattern of growth to that in current spending on content and material. The largest rise over the two-year period was in Finland. Expenditure fell in Spain as well as in the UK, where outlays on content and services increased substantially. Capital outlays rose by much more in Germany, where the rise in current spending was modest, than in either Italy or the Netherlands (Figure 28).

There is enough evidence the market for capital equipment can behave differently from that for e-learning material and training content. This stresses the importance of treating the two separately in any survey or analysis. Please note, however, the arrival of learning content management systems (LCMS) and integrated services blurs this distinction. This difference, and the lack of growth in spending on e-learning material in several countries, supports evidence that developing e-learning content, and software rather than hardware, has not kept pace with the potential of equipment, and technology in general, to deliver new forms of training and new ways of teaching.

3.5. Growth of revenue and expenditure by size of organisation

Figure 29: E-learning as a share of revenue from supply of training material and share of current expenditure on training material by size of organisation

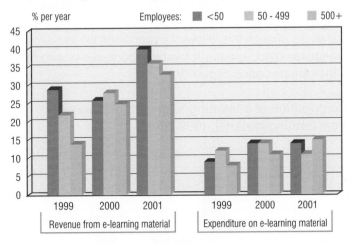

According to the survey, small organisations with fewer than 50 employees involved in supplying training material gained a larger share of their revenue from e-learning-related content than larger ones (40 % as opposed to 33 % in organisations with 500 or more employees). This is in line with their greater use of e-learning methods in delivering training, noted above. Nevertheless, small organisations experienced much less of an increase in the relative amount of revenue from e-learning than larger ones over the two years 1999 and 2001 (Figure 29).

Figure 30: **Growth of revenue from e-learning material and current and capital expenditure on e-learning by size of organisation, 1999-2001**

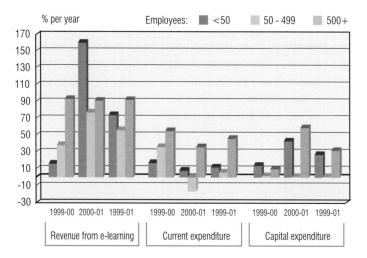

Despite this, small concerns estimated that they were likely to achieve a much higher rate of growth of revenue from e-learning content in 2001 than larger organisations, though this followed a year when the increase in revenue from e-learning was much greater for large organisations with 500 or more employees than smaller ones (Figure 30).

Figure 31: **Contribution of e-learning to growth of revenue from training material, 1999-2001**

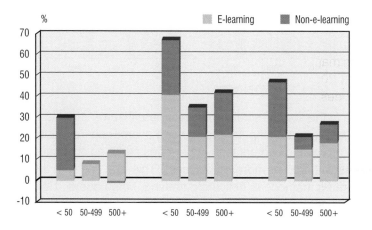

E-learning, however, made a bigger contribution to overall revenue growth from supplying training content or services in large organisations than small ones over the two-year period as a whole. This reflects the increase in the share of revenue from such methods noted above. While in organisations employing 500 or more people – and, indeed, in those employing 50 to 499 – e-learning-related content accounted for over 70 % of the overall increase in revenue from training over the two years, in those employing fewer than 50, a much larger proportion of revenue (65 %) was generated by other training activities than by e-learning (Figure 31).

Figure 32: **Contribution of e-learning to growth of expenditure on training material, 1999-2001**

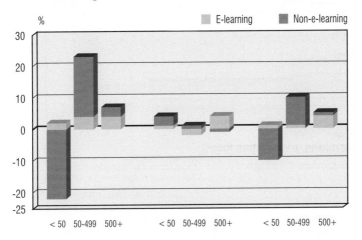

For users, small organisations spent a slightly smaller proportion of their budget for training material on e-learning-related content than large ones (though more than medium-sized concerns). The growth of spending by users on e-learning material was also higher for large organisations than for smaller ones, in both 2000 and 2001. In the latter year, organisations with 500 or more employees estimated an increase in spending of 36 % compared with a rise of 8 % in those with under 50 employees, while those between estimated a decline. Nevertheless, for small organisations, e-learning-related content was the only area of current spending growth over the two years taken together, as it was for large concerns (Figure 32). By contrast, in medium-sized organisations with 50 to 499 employees, spending on other training material contributed much more to expenditure growth than e-learning.

Expenditure on capital equipment for e-learning purposes also increased by more over the period in large organisations than small ones, though the difference was less marked.

3.6. Growth of revenue and expenditure by type of organisation

Figure 33: **E-learning as a share of revenue from supply of training material by type of organisation, 1999, 2000 and 2001**

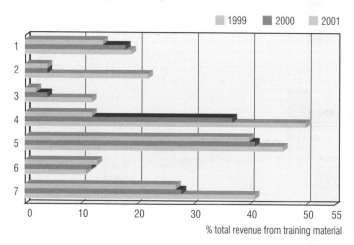

1 University/college
2 Public vocational education and training organisation
3 Sector/industry training body
4 Voluntary/social organisation
5 Private training company
6 Private/public organisation with internal and external training
7 Specialist producing tools/content

The importance of e-learning as a source of revenue differs significantly between organisations of different types. In 2001, e-learning material was responsible for half the revenue from training in voluntary organisations responding to the survey, reflecting the considerable increase over the preceding two years, and for some 46 % in private training companies (Figure 33). By contrast, it accounted for only 19 % of revenue in respect of universities and colleges and for only around 11 to 12 % of industry or sector training bodies and non-specialist organisations with internal and external training, though in training bodies, it had risen markedly in 2001.

Figure 34: **Contribution of e-learning to growth of revenue from supply of training material, 1999-2001**

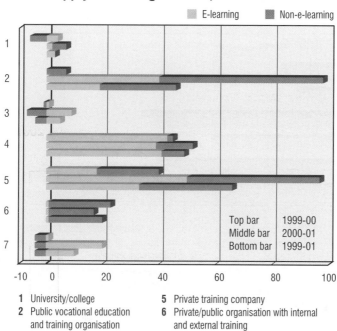

Top bar	1999-00
Middle bar	2000-01
Bottom bar	1999-01

1 University/college
2 Public vocational education and training organisation
3 Sector/industry training body
4 Voluntary/social organisation
5 Private training company
6 Private/public organisation with internal and external training
7 Specialist producing tools/content

In organisations of all types, except non-specialist ones providing training both internally and externally, the share of total revenue from e-learning increased over the two years 1999 to 2001. Therefore, e-learning was responsible for most of the growth in revenue over the period in four of the seven types of organisation for which data are available for enough respondents (Figure 34). Among the exceptions were private training companies, for which other training activities were still a more important source of revenue growth. (This may reflect changes over the period which are calculated only for respondents giving data for adjacent years and are, therefore, more likely to exclude newcomers to the training market than traditional suppliers.)

Figure 35: **E-learning as a share of current expenditure on training material by type of organisation, 1999, 2000, 2001**

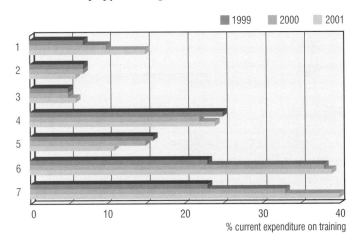

1   University/college
2   Public vocational education and training organisation
3   Sector/industry training body
4   Voluntary/social organisation
5   Private training company
6   Private/public organisation with internal and external training
7   Specialist producing tools/content

The growth of spending on e-learning material by different types of organisation shows a different picture. Only in non-specialist organisations involved in both internal and external training and specialist companies producing tools or content did e-learning account for more than a quarter of total current spending on training. In the public sector, vocational education and training organisations and industry or sector training bodies, it represented only around 6 % (Figure 35).

Figure 36: **Contribution of spending on e-learning material to growth of current expenditure on training, 1999-2001**

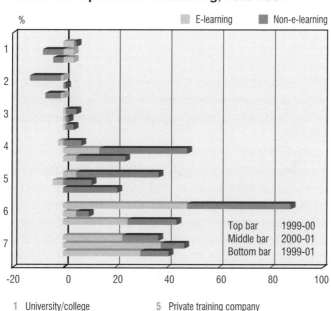

1 University/college
2 Public vocational education and training organisation
3 Sector/industry training body
4 Voluntary/social organisation
5 Private training company
6 Private/public organisation with internal and external training
7 Specialist producing tools/content

Also, in the former, the proportion declined over the two years 1999 to 2001, while in the latter, there was only a modest increase. There was also a decline in the proportion of expenditure on e-learning-related material in voluntary organisations and a much larger fall in private training companies, where the share of spending going on e-learning declined from 15.5 % to 10.5 %. In the three types of organisation, however, particularly in universities and specialist companies producing content, the proportion increased markedly. In universities e-learning was the only area of spending growth over the two years. In specialist companies it accounted for almost 75 % of the overall increase in expenditure (Figure 36).

4. Summary of main findings

The conclusions to be drawn from the survey provide a valuable insight into the nature of the e-learning market and the way it is developing. They also throw light on the feasibility of collecting data by a direct approach to participants in the market.

Although the primary aim of the study on which this report is based was not to assemble a representative set of data, many organisations in the EU have provided information about the use of e-learning in vocational education and training and professional development in the EU. While it is impossible to ascertain how far these are representative of the concerns involved in vocational education and training, whether as suppliers or users, they, nevertheless, include different types and sizes of organisation from all EU countries.

The results show that such an approach, by exploiting the potential of the Internet, can produce valuable information within a relatively short period of time without incurring large-scale costs.

The experience of this exercise suggests that it ought to be possible to collect information of this kind regularly to monitor developments in e-learning, and indeed, in initial and continuing training more generally.

The results of the survey confirm the importance of distinguishing between countries in the EU, between the demand and supply sides of the market and between current expenditure on training material and capital spending on equipment and infrastructure. The main findings are:

- Almost 20 % of the organisations located in the EU that responded to the survey were not involved in e-learning at all, either as suppliers or users, despite being either providers or consumers of vocational education and training.
- The proportion of respondents not involved in e-learning varied significantly between EU countries, from none at all in Finland and few in Sweden to around a quarter in Greece, almost 30 % in France and Austria, over a third in Belgium and over 40 % in Portugal. This is indicative of the less extensive use of e-learning techniques in the latter countries.
- Some 60 % of all those involved in e-learning in the EU, were both suppliers and users of e-learning. As in the academic publishing market, therefore, most of those producing e-learning content or equipment are also consumers of such content or equipment.

- In all countries, except Belgium, most users of e-learning for training purposes were also suppliers, the figure reaching almost 75 % in Sweden and nearly 70 % in Denmark.
- Large organisations involved in training are more likely to supply or use e-learning than smaller ones and are also more likely to be both users and suppliers, though, at the same time, small organisations involved in e-learning rely on it more than larger organisations and make less use of classroom tuition.
- Most of the different types of organisation involved in vocational education and training, whether as users or suppliers, make some use of e-learning – over 90 % of specialist companies producing training tools or content and organisations only with internal training, around 85 % of universities or colleges and private training companies and almost 80 % of public sector vocational education and training organisations and sector training bodies.
- On average, around 30 % of time spent by users on training in the EU involved e-learning, though this varied from around half in Sweden and 40 % in Greece and Italy to only around 20 % in Denmark, Germany and Portugal and 15 % in Belgium. These figures reflect variations in the extent and characteristics of vocational education and training between countries as well as the use of e-learning methods in itself.
- E-learning and classroom-based methods of training are not necessarily alternatives to each other and may be complementary. While for suppliers of training, greater use of e-learning goes with less use of classroom-based methods, for users, this is much less the case and the two are combined in different ways in different countries.
- There is some variation in the use made of e-learning for training in different subject areas. It was highest in information and communication technology, where some 43 % of time spent by those receiving training involved e-learning methods and lowest, but still significant, in processing and production and sales and marketing, in both of which the figure was 24 %.
- E-learning was estimated by training suppliers to be responsible for around a third of their total income from the supply of training content and material in 2001. This was markedly higher than two years previously, when it was the source of just over 18 % of total income, reflecting substantial growth in revenue from e-learning over the period (estimated at an average of 70 % a year).
- For suppliers of capital equipment and infrastructure, e-learning-related sales accounted for an average of 23 % of total income in 2001, up from 19 % in 1999.

- Small organisations involved in supplying training material earned a larger share of their income from e-learning-related content than larger ones, in line with the greater use of e-learning in delivering training. The share of large organisations, however, increased by more in the two years 1999 to 2001.
- For users, e-learning-related investment is estimated to have been responsible for almost 13 % of their expenditure on capital equipment for training in 2001, much the same as in 1999 and lower than in 2000, despite significant growth in spending.
- Some 14 % of total spending by users of training went on e-learning-related content in 2001, appreciably more than two years earlier when the figure was under 10 %.
- In 2000, spending on e-learning material by users increased by just over 40 %, while other current spending on training rose by only 3 %. In 2001, however, the growth in spending on e-learning is estimated to have fallen to 14 %, while current outlays on other forms of training is also thought to have fallen.
- The slowdown in the growth of expenditure on e-learning in 2001 reflects the economic slowdown in the EU, suggesting the market like others is not immune to underlying conditions in the economy.
- The big difference between the rate of growth in the e-learning market estimated by suppliers and users proves the importance of examining both sides of the market when assessing prospects.
- In all EU countries, apart from Spain where it has declined, the proportion of total expenditure on training going to e-learning methods increased in the two years 1999 to 2001, though the growth in spending varied from almost 100 % a year in Finland to 9 % a year in Germany.

5. Survey methods and questionnaire

The questionnaire reproduced below, was designed to cover the main points at issue as concisely as possible. It was divided into four sections:

- classification of respondents by country, type and size of organisation to filter the data provided for analysis (see questionnaire for a list of specified types and size ranges);
- information on organisations as suppliers and/or users of e-learning for internal and external training purposes;
- the extent of e-learning-based and classroom-based training in selected subject areas (see questionnaire for a list of these);
- revenue and expenditure on vocational education and training as a whole and within this on e-learning specifically in 1999, 2000 and 2001. A distinction was made between training content or material (software, Internet use, wages and salaries of trainers and so on) and the infrastructure and equipment – or hardware – for training. This is important not only to gain an insight into the two parts of the market but to avoid aggregating current expenditure and capital investment, which can be misleading, since investment is intended for use over several years rather than being specific to the current one. However, the distinction between buying CD-ROMs, which would typically be booked as current expenditure, and a PC, which would be booked as capital, is questionable.) Respondents were asked first to indicate the overall revenue and costs associated with training by broad monetary band and within this the proportion for e-learning.

A final section of the survey asked respondents to supply contact details with the incentive that by doing so they would receive a summary of the survey results.

5.1. Survey deployment

The survey was conducted through the Internet, the questionnaire hosted on the website of the European Training Village (ETV www.trainingvillage.gr) of Cedefop. The questionnaire was in four languages - English, French, German and Spanish. –to encourage as many respondents as possible to complete it. Completed questionnaires were then collected and processed using a third party polling server (InfoPoll).

Notice of the survey and requests to complete the questionnaire were sent to contact e-mail addresses of those involved in training. These were obtained both from existing databases, starting with the Cedefop contact list, and from direct investigation in the countries selected for special attention (the five largest EU Member States, Greece, the Netherlands and Finland). Initial e-mail requests were followed up by a reminder sent one week later.

The first phase of the survey involved e-mail notice to 12 000 or so registered members of the ETV, mainly based in the EU but also include some from other parts of Europe and the rest of the world. This produced over 550 responses, a response rate of around 4.5 %, which is close to that of previous web-based surveys on training conducted by Cedefop.

The second phase focused on the eight Member States listed above. For this phase, several databases were identified and used, including the vocational education and training institute database held by Cedefop and the European Commission Leonardo da Vinci partner search database.

5.2. The questionnaire

This survey, commissioned by Cedefop, represents the first major attempt to assess the current extent of e-learning(*) within vocational and professional education and training in Europe. By completing this short survey a significant contribution to understanding and measuring the e-learning market will be made. Once completed, all respondents may receive a summary of the survey results - see Section 6 below.

All information provided by any individual/organisation will be confidential and noone other than those responsible for carrying out the survey will have access to the information provided by individual respondents.

(*) e-learning is any training provided by electronic media, whether through CD-ROM or accessing an online service.

5.2.1. **About your organisation**

Where is your organisation based?
Please choose a region and specify country

European Union	Other Europe	Other (please specify)
Belgium	Albania	
Denmark	Bosnia & Herzegovina	
Germany	Bulgaria	
Greece	Croatia	
Spain	Cyprus	
France	Czech Republic	
Ireland	Estonia	
Italy	FYROM	
Luxembourg	Hungary	
Netherlands	Iceland	
Austria	Latvia	
Portugal	Lithuania	
Finland	Malta	
Sweden	Norway	
United Kingdom	Poland	
	Romania	
	Slovenia	
	Slovakia	
	Switzerland	
	Yugoslavia	
	Other	

How would you classify your organisation?
- ❑ University, college of further/higher education or equivalent
- ❑ Public vocational education and training organisation
- ❑ Sector/industry training body (organised
  by professional/trade association, trade union)
- ❑ Voluntary or social organisation
- ❑ Private training company/organisation
- ❑ Private or public organisation (any sector)
  with internal training services
- ❑ Private or public organisation (any sector)
  with internal and external training services
- ❑ Organisation specialising in producing/providing training tools/content
- ❑ Other. Please specify

What is the approximate annual turnover of your organisation?
Please specify in either USD or EUR

Approximately how many people are employed in your organisation?

- ❑ <20
- ❑ 20-49
- ❑ 50-99
- ❑ 100-249
- ❑ 250-499
- ❑ 500-999
- ❑ 1000+

5.2.2. E-learning users

Are you a supplier and/or user of e-learning?
Please indicate whether e-learning is supplied and/or used internally within your organisation, externally to another organisation or both.

	Internally	Externally	Both
Supplier of e-learning			
User/purchaser of e-learning			
Both supply and use e-learning			
Neither supply nor use e-learning			

5.2.3. Subject areas and methods of delivery

Suppliers of training
What percentage of the following subject areas do you provide
by classroom and by e-learning?

	% classroom learning hours	% e-learning learning hours
Information technology/computing		
Technical(non-IT)		
Language learning		
Management		
Process/production training		
Sales/marketing		
Teamwork/communications		
Quality		
New product/service training		
Other		

Users/purchasers of training
What percentage of your requirements for the following subject areas is by classroom and by e-learning?

	% classroom learning hours	% e-learning learning hours
Information technology/computing		
Technical(non-IT)		
Language learning		
Management		
Process/production training		
Sales/marketing		
Teamwork/communications		
Quality		
New product/service training		
Other		

5.2.4. Suppliers of training - Revenue from e-learning

Please estimate the actual and expected revenue from all training and e-learning supplied by your organisation, distinguishing between:
(a) revenue from supplying training materials/programmes;
(b) revenue from sale of capital equipment (i.e. on infrastructure, including PCs, networks, etc.).

Total revenue from all training supplied by your organisation
Please specify in either euro (EUR) or US dollars (USD)

Revenue from supplying materials/programmes (EUR or USD)

EUR or USD	in 1999	in 2000	in 2001
< 100 000			
100 000-500 000			
500 000-1 million			
1-5 million			
5-10 million			
10-20 million			
20 million+			

Revenue from supplying capital equipment (EUR or USD)

EUR or USD	in 1999	in 2000	in 2001
< 100 000			
100 000-500 000			
500 000-1 million			
1-5 million			
5-10 million			
10-20 million			
20 million+			

What proportion of the total revenue from training supplied by your organisation is accounted for by e-learning?
In % of total revenue from all training supplied by your organisation given above

Revenue from supplying materials/programmes

EUR or USD	in 1999	in 2000	in 2001
< 10 %			
10-20 %			
20-30 %			
30-40 %			
40-50 %			
50-60 %			
60-70 %			
70-80 %			
80-90 %			
90-100 %			

Revenue from supplying capital equipment

EUR or USD	in 1999	in 2000	in 2001
< 10 %			
10-20 %			
20-30 %			
30-40 %			
40-50 %			
50-60 %			
60-70 %			
70-80 %			
80-90 %			
90-100 %			

5.2.5. Users/purchasers of training - Expenditure on e-learning

Please estimate your organisation's actual and planned expenditure on training and e-learning, distinguishing between:

(a) operating costs for delivery of training (including wages and salaries, purchase of material/courses, software, communication costs, subscription to websites, etc.);

(b) capital costs of training (i.e. on infrastructure, including PCs, networks, etc.).

Total training expenditure
Please specify in either EUR or USD

Operating costs

EUR or USD	in 1999	in 2000	in 2001
< 100 000			
100 000-500 000			
500 000-1 million			
1-5 million			
5-10 million			
10-20 million			
20 million+			

Capital costs

EUR or USD	in 1999	in 2000	in 2001
< 100 000			
100 000-500 000			
500 000-1 million			
1-5 million			
5-10 million			
10-20 million			
20 million+			

What proportion of total training expenditure is on e-learning?
In % of total training expenditure given above

Operating costs

EUR or USD	in 1999	in 2000	in 2001
< 10 %			
10-20 %			
20-30 %			
30-40 %			
40-50 %			
50-60 %			
60-70 %			
70-80 %			
80-90 %			
90-100 %			

Capital costs

EUR or USD	in 1999	in 2000	in 2001
< 10 %			
10-20 %			
20-30 %			
30-40 %			
40-50 %			
50-60 %			
60-70 %			
70-80 %			
80-90 %			
90-100 %			

5.2.6. **Obtaining survey results**

If you would like to receive (by e-mail) a summary of the results of this survey, then please complete the contact details below.

Contact information (optional)
All information provided by any individual/organisation will be confidential and no one other than those responsible for carrying out the survey will have access to the information provided by individual respondents. This contact information will not be disclosed or passed on to anyone else.

❑ Your name
❑ Title
❑ E-mail address
❑ Name of organisation

6. Recent studies on e-learning in Europe

Corporate e-learning – Realising the potential

Xebec McGraw-Hill; Training Magazine, October 2001
http://www.xebec-online.com/new/trngtalk/resources/pdfs/survey2001results.pdf

Sample UK
334 responses

Nature of survey Demand and supply-side analysis. Direct surveying of *Training magazine* readers, plus other training and human resource professionals.

Issues covered
- Respondent profile by job type, number of employees, number of training specialists, business sector and number of sites
- Use of intranet/Internet to deliver training now and within three years, by firm size and business sector
- E-learning budgets for 2000, 2001 and 2002
- Types of e-learning support used
- Use of e-learning in the training mix
- Evaluation of e-learning

Principal results
- 28% of companies with intranets use them to deliver training and a further 54% will do so in three years. 24% of companies use the Internet to deliver training and 46% will do so in three years.
- Almost 80% of organisations with corporate intranets use them to deliver information and communication technology skills
- Information and communication technology, chemicals/ pharmaceuticals, communications/media and finance business sectors have adopted e-learning most quickly
- 58% of organisations spending less than 10% of their training budgets on e-learning; 12% of e-learning users will spend >25% of their training budget on e-learning in the coming year
- Over 90% of organisations delivering online training also carry out evaluation of the effectiveness of this method of learning

E-learning and the UK IT training market

OVUM, September 2001
Http://www.ovum.com/go/product/flyer/HLL.htm

Sample	UK
	IT training sector only, sample size unknown

Nature of survey Supply-side only. Analysis of major e-learning vendors in UK.
Forecasts for 2001-04.

Issues covered
- E-learning strategies
- Value-added training services
- Learning management systems
- Market size and forecast
- Leading suppliers of IT training to the UK market
- Industry dynamics
- International markets

Principal results
- E-learning will account for 20% of UK IT training market by 2004
- Overall IT training market to grow at 6% per year over period 2001-04
- Adopts fairly narrow definition of e-learning: Internet-delivered training and reports that growth in this area is slow

E-learning: survey June 2001

RH Info, July 2001
http://www.rhinfo.com/servlet/com.rhinfo.home.doc.printDoc?ID_DOCUMENT=966&ID_LOCATION=1143

Sample France / 194 responses

Nature of survey Demand and supply-side analysis of human resources managers.

Issues covered
- Extent of e-learning use
- Main reasons for adopting e-learning methods
- Degree to which e-learning should be delivered in conjunction with traditional forms of training
- Factors delaying adoption of e-learning
- Provision/use of intranet/Internet learning in the organisation
- Cost savings associated with e-learning
- Share of training budget going to e-learning now and in two years time

Principal results
- E-learning use was just under 24%
- Over 80% believe e-learning should complement traditional training methods
- Non take-up of e-learning due mainly to users being unready to try new learning methods
- Only 11% of companies have an e-learning solution in place
- Of those who had adopted e-learning solutions, a quarter saw no cost saving and a fifth saw savings of less than 10%
- Currently 58% of companies spend less than 5% of their training budgets on e-learning and a further 35% spend between 5% and 30%. In two years' time only 25% will spend less than 5%, 51% will spend between 5% and 30% and 24% will spend more than 30%

European e-learning market forecast and analysis, 2000-05

IDC, July 2001
http://www.itresearch.com/alfatst4.nsf/UNITABSX/WTT03H?OpenDocument

Sample   Western Europe, sample size unknown

Nature of survey Supply-side only. Analysis of major vendors in Europe.
                      Forecasts for 2001-05.

Issues covered   • Main drivers behind e-learning
                      • Product and pricing trends
                      • Market segmentation and forecast by content and country
                      • Major e-learning players in Europe
                      • Main e-learning subjects

Principal results • European e-learning market forecast to be worth USD 6 billion
                        by 2005
                      • By 2005 e-learning will account for a quarter of the European
                        IT training market
                      • European e-learning market will grow by 126% in 2001 alone

'Efficient learning': e-learning and efficient training

Arthur Andersen, March 2001
http://www.andersen.com/Resource2.nsf/AssetsByDescription/e-learning_es_0301%20FRENCH/ $File/e-learning_es_0301.pdf

Sample   France / 74 responses

Nature of survey Demand-side analysis of e-learning users. Questionnaires sent out to directors of the 500 largest French companies; 74 responses

Issues covered   • Overall spending on training plus forecasts for following two years
                      • Share of enterprises using e-learning (incl. CD-ROM, intranet, Internet)
                      • Advantages of e-learning
                      • Factors delaying the adoption of e-learning
                      • Factors affecting the successful take-up of e-learning
                      • Criteria for good e-learning content
                      • Satisfaction with e-learning methods used

Principal results • 60% of enterprises responding had used e-learning in 2001 (up from 10.8% in 2000)
                      • Of these 53% had used CD-ROM (30% in 2000); 32% an Internet site (22% in 2000); and 12% an intranet site (no change from 2000)
                      • Sectors using Internet and intranet most are banking, industry and insurance
                      • No link between size of enterprise and take-up of e-learning

Nordic corporate e-learning market, 2000-05

IDC, January 2001
http://www.itresearch.com/alfatst4.nsf/UNITABSX/WN560100H?OpenDocument

Sample   Sweden, Denmark, Finland, Norway, sample size unknown

Nature of survey   Supply-side only. Analysis of major vendors in Nordic countries. Forecasts for 2000-05.

Issues covered
- Main drivers and e-learning industry trends
- Product and pricing trends
- Market segmentation and forecast by content and country
- Major e-learning players by type of vendor
- Anatomy of an e-learning system

Principal results
- Nordic corporate e-learning market forecast to grow by 71% between 2000 and 2005

Attitudes to e-learning: a national survey 2000

Campaign forlearning; KPMG; Ufi Ltd; Peter Honey Learning, 2000
http://www.campaign-for-learning.org.uk/news/e-learning.htm

Sample   UK / 183 Individual learners; 44 employer budget holders; 103 e-learning providers' responses

Nature of survey   Demand and supply-side analysis. Direct surveying. Three separate question-naires examining the practice and attitudes towards e-learning of: individual e-learners; employer budget holders for e-learning; providers of e-learning.

Issues covered
- E-learning environments and preferred methods for e-learning
- Involvement with - and quality of - formal and informal e-learning
- Advantages/disadvantages of e-learning
- E-learning budgets
- E-learning products and services

Principal results
- Most e-learning occurs in the workplace, although a third of individuals do most of their learning at home
- Almost all e-learners feel a need for learning support, though less than two-thirds of employers offer such support
- Employers deliver e-learning mainly through purchasing existing products, asking employees to conduct web searches and developing in-house materials
- The majority of employers spend less than 5% of training budgets on e-learning
- Almost a quarter of employers remain undecided about the potential of e-learning
- Employers and e-learning providers see e-learning as being advantageous as it reduces tutor contact time and time spent off the job
- Both employers and providers believe that e-learning needs to be further developed to replace other forms of training, though neither believes the future lies solely with e-learning

Corporate foundations for e-learning success

Xebec McGraw-Hill; Training Magazine, October 2000
http://www.xebec-online.com/new/trngtalk/resources/pdfs/survey2000.pdf

Sample UK / 498 responses

Nature of survey Demand and supply-side analysis. Direct surveying of *Training magazine* readers, plus other training and human resource professionals.

Issues covered
- Respondent profile by job type, number of employees, number of training specialists, business sector and number of sites
- Use of intranet/Internet to deliver training now and within three years, by firm size and business sector
- Barriers to the implementation of online training
- The effect of online learning on trainers

Principal results
- 28% of companies with intranets use them to deliver training and a further 48% will do so in three years
- 18% of companies use the Internet to deliver training and 42% will do so in three years
- Two thirds of those using online training do so for information and communication technology skills
- Effective delivery of online training is hindered by interruptions at the desktop. Both this and successful implementation of online training is affected by lack of commitment from senior management

European corporate e-learning: market forecast and analysis 2000

IDC, October 2000
http://emea.idc.com/press/20010105.htm

Sample Western Europe, Sample size unknown

Nature of survey Supply-side only. Analysis of major vendors in Europe. Produces forecast for 2000-04.

Issues covered
- Main drivers and e-learning industry trends
- Product and pricing trends
- Market segmentation and forecast by content and country
- Major e-learning players in Europe
- Main e-learning subjects
- Anatomy of an e-learning system

Principal results
- European e-learning market forecast to be worth USD 4 billion by 2004, this represents growth of 96% a year over the period 2000-04
- By 2004 over half of e-learning will be IT training, the rest will be soft skills (sales, marketing and leadership skills)
- Content is the largest component of the e-learning market
- UK, Netherlands and Sweden main adopters of e-learning due to higher levels of Internet penetration and use of English

E-learning: survey September 2000

RH Info, October 2000
http://www.rhinfo.com/servlet/com.rhinfo.home.doc.printDoc?ID_DOCUMENT=695&ID_LOCATION=852

Sample   France / 364 responses

Nature of survey Demand and supply-side analysis of human resources managers.

Issues covered
- Willingness/readiness of company/employees to use e-learning methods
- Degree to which e-learning should be delivered in conjunction with traditional forms of training
- Main reason for adopting e-learning
- Factors delaying adoption of e-learning
- Degree to which e-learning forms part of training policy within enterprise
- Types of training to be tried out with e-learning methods
- Share of training budget given to e-learning now and in two years' time

Principal results
- 48% believe company/employee mentality not yet ready to adopt e-learning methods
- Cost savings are the main attraction of using e-learning
- 45% spend less than 5% of their training budgets on e-learning and 35% spend between 5% and 30%; in two years' time only 12% will spend less than 5% and more than half will spend over 30% of their training budget on e-learning.

7. List of figures

Cedefop (European Centre for the Development of Vocational Training)

E-learning and training in Europe

**A survey into the use of e-learning
in training and professional development
in the European Union**

Luxembourg:
Office for Official Publications of the European Communities

2002 – VI, 65 pp. – 17.5 x 25 cm

(Cedefop Reference series; 26 – ISSN 1608-7089)

ISBN 92-896-0106-X

Cat. No: TI-41-01-931-EN-C

Price (excluding VAT) in Luxembourg: EUR 40

No of publication: 3021 EN